ECK Essentials

Your Keys to Spiritual Living

Also by Harold Klemp

Animals Are Soul Too!
The Art of Spiritual Dreaming
Ask the Master, Books 1 and 2
Autobiography of a Modern Prophet
The Call of Soul
A Cosmic Sea of Words: The ECKANKAR Lexicon
ECKANKAR's Spiritual Experiences Guidebook
ECK Masters and You: An Illustrated Guide
ECK Wisdom Temples, Spiritual Cities, & Guides: A Brief History
Is Life a Random Walk?
A Modern Prophet Answers Your Key Questions about Life, Books 1 and 2
Past Lives, Dreams, and Soul Travel
The Sound of Soul
The Spiritual Exercises of ECK
The Spiritual Laws of Life
Those Wonderful ECK Masters
Youth Ask a Modern Prophet about Life, Love, and God

The Mahanta Transcripts Series
Journey of Soul, Book 1
How to Find God, Book 2
The Secret Teachings, Book 3
The Golden Heart, Book 4
Cloak of Consciousness, Book 5
Unlocking Your Sacred Puzzle Box, Book 6
The Eternal Dreamer, Book 7
The Dream Master, Book 8
We Come as Eagles, Book 9
The Drumbeat of Time, Book 10
What Is Spiritual Freedom? Book 11
How the Inner Master Works, Book 12
The Slow Burning Love of God, Book 13
The Secret of Love, Book 14
Our Spiritual Wake-Up Calls, Book 15
How to Survive Spiritually in Our Times, Book 16
The Road to Spiritual Freedom, Book 17

The Immortality of Soul Series
The Awakened Heart
The Awakening Soul
HU, the Most Beautiful Prayer
The Language of Soul
Love—The Keystone of Life
The Loving Heart
The Spiritual Life
Touching the Face of God
Truth Has No Secrets

ECK Wisdom Series
ECK Wisdom on Conquering Fear
ECK Wisdom on Dreams
ECK Wisdom on Inner Guidance
ECK Wisdom on Karma and Reincarnation
ECK Wisdom on Life after Death
ECK Wisdom on Solving Problems

Spiritual Wisdom Series
Spiritual Wisdom on Health and Healing
Spiritual Wisdom on Prayer, Meditation, and Contemplation
Spiritual Wisdom on Relationships

Stories to Help You See God in Your Life
The Book of ECK Parables, Volumes 1, 2, and 3
Stories to Help You See God in Your Life, ECK Parables, Book 4

 This book has been authored by and published under the supervision of the Mahanta, the Living ECK Master, Sri Harold Klemp. It is the Word of ECK.

ECK Essentials

Your Keys to Spiritual Living

HAROLD KLEMP

ECKANKAR
Minneapolis
www.Eckankar.org

ECK Essentials

Copyright © 2018 ECKANKAR

All rights reserved. No part of this book may be reproduced, stored in a retrieval system, or transmitted in any form by any means, whether electronic, mechanical, photocopying, recording, or otherwise, without prior written permission of Eckankar.

The terms ECKANKAR, ECK, EK, MAHANTA, SOUL TRAVEL, and VAIRAGI, among others, are trademarks of ECKANKAR, PO Box 2000, Chanhassen, MN 55317-2000 USA.   171237

Printed in USA

ISBN: 978-1-57043-462-4

Edited by Patrick Carroll, Joan Klemp, and Anthony Moore

Photo of Sri Harold Klemp (pages viii and 77) by Art Galbraith

Cover Art by Melony Mont-Eton

Text illustrations by Ron Wennekes

Library of Congress Cataloging-in-Publication Data

Names: Klemp, Harold, author.
Title: ECK essentials : your keys to spiritual living / Harold Klemp.
Description: Minneapolis : ECKANKAR, 2018.
Identifiers: LCCN 2018007813 | ISBN 9781570434624 (pbk. : alk. paper)
Subjects: LCSH: Eckankar (Organization)--Doctrines.
Classification: LCC BP605.E3 K55368 2018 | DDC 299/.93--dc23 LC record available at https://lccn.loc.gov/2018007813

∞ This paper meets the requirements of ANSI/NISO Z39.48-1992 (Permanence of Paper).

Contents

Introduction 1

Wisdoms of ECK
Essential Spiritual Basics

Two Supreme Laws ❧ The Purpose of Life ❧ Your State of Consciousness ❧ Purify or Pollute ❧ Soul Equals Soul ❧ True Necessary Kind ❧ Richard Maybury's Two Laws ❧ Your Golden Contract ❧ God in Expression ❧ Vairag ❧ The Splendor of Soul

Heartsongs of ECK
Essential Truths to Live By

The Mahanta 13
Three Basic Principles of Eckankar 14
Three Eternal Principles of Eckankar 15
Jewels of ECK 15
Four Fundamentals of ECK 16
Four Disciplines of ECK 18
Four Precepts of ECK 20
Four Points on How to Serve the ECK 21
The Purpose of the Kal Power 22
Four Zoas 22
Four States of the High Initiate 24

Five Points to Master Your Spiritual Destiny 26
Five Spiritual Laws of This World 28
Five Passions of the Mind 29
Five Virtues 32
Five Keys to ECK Mastership 34
Seven Margs 35
The Council of the Nine 37
Twelve-Year Cycles of the Master's Spiritual Mission 38
The Spiritual Years of ECK 41
The Creation of Life 48
Liberation of HU 49
Goodness like Water 50
The Master's Gift 51
Every Moment 52
Lai Tsi's Prayer 53
Marks of the ECK Leader 54

ECK Parables

Essential Stories to Live By

The Scratched Diamond 59
"Turn the Carpet" or "The Two Weavers" 62
The Zen Master 65
The Master Brush Cleaner 67
"One Does What One Can" 69

The Jade Master 70
The God Seeker 74

               ও   ও   ও

About the Author 77
Advanced Spiritual Living 78
For Further Reading and Study 80
Glossary 82

Sri Harold Klemp
The Mahanta, the Living ECK Master

Introduction

Welcome, spiritual traveler!

Whether you are taking your first bold steps into the God worlds of your being, or you are a seasoned traveler in the ways of ECK, these essential truths and touchstones will serve as a ready spiritual compass.

Each precept, law or parable, key or contemplation seed, holds a myriad of truths for Soul.

Spend some quality time with the Inner Master as you explore these pages, and he will reveal their truths—not only what lies on the page, but all between the lines and its relevance to your life today.

It's more than you think.

Visit this book every so often for new levels of insight as Soul continues to refine Its agreements with the ECK.

Listen and look within. The Mahanta is holding open the doors of Soul, so let's get started!

Harold Klemp

Wisdoms of ECK

Essential Spiritual Basics

Two Supreme Laws

The two supreme laws are: God is love, and Soul exists because God loves It.

—Adapted from *How to Survive Spiritually in Our Times*, Mahanta Transcripts, Book 16, p. 215

How have you experienced God's love for Soul today?

The Purpose of Life

What is the purpose of life? Why are we here? It is to learn to give and receive God's love.

—*Our Spiritual Wake-Up Calls*, Mahanta Transcripts, Book 15, p. 21

Let the Mahanta show you a new way to give love. What did you receive?

Your State of Consciousness

Your state of consciousness is your state of acceptance.

This means that someone who has a very open state of consciousness is able to accept more of what life has to offer—not just the hardships, but also the blessings and love that come to each individual.

—Adapted from *How to Survive Spiritually in Our Times*, Mahanta Transcripts, Book 16, pp. 114–15

Make a postulate. Say, "I will open myself to a greater acceptance of love, blessings, and responsibility."

Purify or Pollute

Every thought, word, or deed either purifies or pollutes the body.

—*The Spiritual Laws of Life*, p. 88

Take this to heart, and make the most of your day. You will find the truth of this principle.

Soul Equals Soul

Every Soul's destiny is spiritual liberation; it's for every Soul. One Soul is not greater or less than another Soul.

—*Be the HU: How to Become a
Co-worker with God*, p. 205

How do you show your respect for others?

True Necessary Kind

The guiding rule that will stand you well throughout life is this ECK saying: Is it true? Is it necessary? Is it kind?

Unless the answer is yes for all three, then you would do well to reconsider your intended action.

—*Youth Ask a Modern Prophet
about Life, Love, and God*, p. 17

There will be something in your day to inspire you to remember this principle.

Richard Maybury's Two Laws

"Do all you have agreed to do" and "Do not encroach on other persons or their property."

—*Our Spiritual Wake-Up Calls*,
Mahanta Transcripts, Book 15, p. 201

Look for the highest truth in these two laws. They are a key to spiritual freedom.

Your Golden Contract

This is the golden contract: that every encounter, without exception, is there to move Soul along spiritually on Its way back home to God. That's every encounter, every event, without exception.

—*The Master's Talks in A Year of Creativity—2009–10*, p. 9

Think about an encounter in your day. How did it help you grow spiritually?

God in Expression

As we go about our day, ideas come through on how to solve problems, how to make our work easier, or how to make things better for someone else.

These ideas come from the creative imagination which, to state it as simply as possible, is God in expression, manifesting Its creation in this world through our actions. This is God speaking through us.

The creative imagination is the element that makes us godlike.

—Adapted from *Unlocking Your Sacred Puzzle Box*, Mahanta Transcripts, Book 6, p. 185

Let God speak through you, and make one thing easier for someone else today.

Vairag

Soul lives forever by giving, not by receiving.

—*A Cosmic Sea of Words: The ECKANKAR Lexicon*, p. 215

Put this truth into your own words, and then practice this as the Inner Master leads you.

The Splendor of Soul

Soul is immortal, and Its future is the future of a thing whose growth and splendor has no limits.

—*The Shariyat-Ki-Sugmad*, Books One & Two, p. 318

Today is a day to experience the growth and splendor of Soul. Look for this natural occurrence.

Heartsongs of ECK

Essential Truths to Live By

The Mahanta

The Mahanta liberates Soul from the grasp of the Kal forces. He is the good that dwells in the heart of every mortal creature. He is the beginning, the life span, and the end of all mortal creatures. He is the radiant sun, the wind, the stars of the night, and the moon. He is the king of heaven, of the sense organs, of the mind, of the consciousness of living. He is the spirit of fire, the spirit of the mountains, leader of all priests, the ocean's spirit, the greater seer; the sacred syllable ECK, the tree, the ant, the thunder in the heavens, and the god of fishes and sharks. He is time and the eagle, the lion and bear, the rivers of the world, the sustainer, the newborn babe, and the old man preparing to die. In all things is his face, and in all life is he the divine seed. In this world, nothing animate or inanimate exists without him. This is the Lord Sugmad in action, and one atom of Its body sustains the worlds upon worlds. Not only is he the king of this world, but in all worlds, all planets, all planes.

—*The Shariyat-Ki-Sugmad*,
Books One & Two, pp. 38–39

(Continued)

Look for the good that dwells in the heart of everyone you meet. How does it bring out the good in you?

Three Basic Principles of Eckankar

First, Soul is eternal; It has no beginning or end. Second, whosoever travels the high path of ECK dwells in the spiritual planes. Third, Soul always lives in the present; It has no past and no future.

—*The Spiritual Laws of Life*, p. 59

What happens when you live consciously in the present moment?

Three Eternal Principles of Eckankar

The three eternal principles of Eckankar are the proper understanding of God, a knowledge of God, and a knowledge of the creation by God.

—*Stranger by the River*, p. 57

How would you describe your understanding of God? Your knowledge of God? Your knowledge of the creation by God? This examination will bring rewarding insights.

Jewels of ECK

Soul is always in eternity, It is always in the present now, It is always in the heavenly state of the Sugmad, and It exists because of God's love for It.

—*A Cosmic Sea of Words:
The ECKANKAR Lexicon*, p. 103

Go about your day knowing you are a beloved child of God.

Four Fundamentals of ECK

The four basic principles behind the practice of Eckankar:

1. Spiritual Exercises of ECK

Spiritual exercises known to the followers of Eckankar, the Path of Spiritual Freedom, which promote the movement of the inner consciousness known as Soul Travel.

2. Contemplation

In Eckankar, a spiritual exercise during which the attention is focused upon some definite spiritual principle, thought, or idea, or upon the Living ECK Master; differs from meditation in that the definite object or vision gives purpose to the focusing of attention, and is active, rather than passive as in meditation.

3. Inner Master

Light and Sound blended; the highest form of all love; the inner form of the Living ECK Master.

(Continued)

4. Self-Discipline

The control of the subjective self; control of the emotional feelings and the imaginative forces.

—Adapted from *A Cosmic Sea of Words: The ECKANKAR Lexicon*, p. 75

Did you know the Inner Master is the highest form of all love? Make these fundamentals the hub of your spiritual life, and you will find all success comes from the heart.

Four Disciplines of ECK

1. Cleanliness of Mind

Let no words which would pollute the air enter into your mind. Look upon everyone as creatures of God, for they, like yourself, are temples who shall eventually become Co-workers with God. Fast continuously from all Kal (negative) thoughts which could infect your mental state and consciousness. Through this you learn the powerful awareness of the presence of the Living ECK Master, who is with you constantly.

2. Patience

This is the greatest discipline of all the spiritual works of ECK. By patience you can endure life, hardships, karmic burdens, slander, and the pricks of pain and disease. Keep your mind steadfastly upon the Light of God, never swerving, never letting up on your attention to the goal of God-Realization.

3. Humility and Chastity

As you come to know these attributes in your life, you learn all your responsibility belongs to God, not to anyone nor anything with-

(Continued)

in this physical realm. Your loved ones, family, and relatives are images of God, mirrored in this worldly life and embodiment to serve the Sugmad, the Supreme Deity. Realize that humility is opposite to the ego. Do not let a false concept of your worth to the Master and to the Sugmad stand in your way to reach the heavenly states. Know that vanity is only a trap of the negative power, the Kal Niranjan, and you will become a fool if you let yourself be enslaved by the Kal.

4. Discrimination

Learn to discriminate between all things, that there is no good nor evil, no beauty nor ugliness, no sin. These are all concepts of the mind, the dual forces in the matter worlds. Once you recognize and understand this, you will then be free of Kal traps. You will be ready to enter into the Kingdom of God, the Ocean of Love and Mercy. You will be the ECK, of Itself.

—*The Spiritual Exercises of ECK*, pp. 179–80

Each of these disciplines lights your path to spiritual freedom. Which one needs your focus today?

༄

Four Precepts of ECK

The precepts which the chela must have imprinted on his heart and mind:

1. There is but one God and Its reality is the Sugmad.

2. The Mahanta, the Living ECK Master is the messenger of the Sugmad in all worlds be they material, psychic, or spiritual.

3. The faithful, those who follow the works of ECK, shall have all the blessings and riches of the heavenly kingdom given unto them.

4. The Shariyat-Ki-Sugmad is the holy book of those who follow Eckankar, and there shall be none above it.

> —*A Cosmic Sea of Words:*
> *The ECKANKAR Lexicon*, p. 75
>
> See also,
>
> —*The Shariyat-Ki-Sugmad*,
> Books One & Two, p. 285

Why is it important to have these imprinted on your heart? Look for the gift of understanding.

Four Points on How to Serve the ECK

First, always clear a path to the ECK teachings for others.

Second, keep your distance; be detached; and be fair in your dealings with others.

Third, serve ECK only out of love.

Fourth, have absolute patience.

You can find a way to always clear a path to the ECK teachings for others, be fair, and serve ECK only out of love; but more than any of these, you need to practice absolute patience. I speak from experience.

—Adapted from *The Drumbeat of Time,*
Mahanta Transcripts, Book 10, pp. 130–32

There is a place and time to practice each of these points every single day. Doing so will bring spiritual strength, both subtle and profound.

The Purpose of the Kal Power

The Sugmad's purpose in establishing the Kal worlds is to train each Soul to reach the perfection of being a Mahdis, an initiate of the Fifth Circle, which is being a Co-worker with the Mahanta, the Living ECK Master.

—*The Shariyat-Ki-Sugmad*, Books One & Two, p. 175

Consider this purpose when you encounter challenges. What are you being trained in today?

Four Zoas

The four Zoas (laws) of Eckankar for the Mahdis, the initiate of the Fifth Circle, are

1. The Mahdis shall not use alcohol, tobacco, or drugs; gamble; or be gluttonous in any way. No Mahdis shall be existent on the animal level. He is a leader, and he must fix his attention above the psychology of the brute.

(Continued)

2. The Mahdis shall not speak with tongue of vanity or deceit or unhappiness, criticize the actions of others, blame others for wrongdoings, quarrel, fight, or inflict injury. He shall at all times be respectful and courteous to his fellow man and show great compassion and happiness.

3. The Mahdis shall have humility, love, and freedom from all bonds of creeds. He shall be free from the laws of karma which snare him with boastfulness and vanity. He shall have love for all people and creatures of the Sugmad.

4. The Mahdis must preach the message of ECK at all times, and prove to the world that he is an example of purity and happiness. He must show that the disciple in the human body must have a Master in the human body.

—*The Spiritual Laws of Life*, p. 165

See also,

—*The Shariyat-Ki-Sugmad*, Books One & Two, pp. 283–84

Each Zoa is an invitation to move closer to your goal, regardless of your initiation level. How do you respect these laws in your life today?

Four States of the High Initiate

Having reached the fifth degree of initiation, it is the duty of the initiate to improve, to spiritualize himself by contemplation. He is supposed to pass through the four following states: First is Salokiam, which signifies the only tie with the lower worlds. In this state Soul seeks to lift Itself, with the assistance of the Mahanta, the Living ECK Master, to the true spiritual worlds and to take Its place in the presence of Divinity Itself; It holds communication with those Souls who have gone before into the regions of eternity and makes use of the body left on earth as an instrument to transcribe, under the permanent form of writing, the sublime teachings It receives in these worlds of true spirituality.

Second is Samipiam, which signifies proximity. By the exercises of contemplation and the disregard of all earthly objects, the knowledge and idea of the Sugmad becomes familiar to It. It becomes farseeing and begins to witness marvels which are not of this world.

Third is Souaroupiam, which signifies resemblance. In this state Soul gradually acquires a perfect resemblance to the ECK and participates in all Its

(Continued)

attributes. It reads the future and the universe has no secrets for It.

*F*ourth is Sayodiyam, identity. Soul finally becomes closely united to the Mahanta, the Living ECK Master. This last transformation takes place only through the death of the physical body, that is to say, the entire disruption of all material ties by translation.

> —*The Shariyat-Ki-Sugmad,* Books One & Two, pp. 410–11

There is always another state of consciousness to explore. Choose something in this excerpt that speaks to you today, and make it your own—take it into contemplation with the Inner Master.

Five Points to Master Your Spiritual Destiny

Point number one: Forget the past, and learn the spiritual lessons of today.

What is your spiritual lesson today?

Point number two: Look for a new way to solve a stubborn problem.

How can you open yourself to a new point of view?

Point number three: Whatever you undertake, do it to the best of your ability. If necessary, do it even better.

Try this today, and build on your success.

Point number four: Being different can make you an outcast or a leader. Sometime you need to make a choice.

How can you choose to be a leader?

(Continued)

Point number five: Tell others about the teachings of ECK.

Look for new ways to take this step toward Mastership.

—Adapted from *Our Spiritual Wake-Up Calls*, Mahanta Transcripts, Book 15, pp. 74–83

Five Spiritual Laws of This World

These are just five of the many spiritual laws of this world. They are important especially when looking at political and religious fields.

1. The beginning of human life is when breath comes into the fetus.
2. Love is the first and great commandment; also called the rule of spiritual law: love God, love your neighbor, and love yourself.
3. Work for your food. This deals with the welfare system and our responsibility to make our own way as much as we can in this world.
4. Give tribute to God and Caesar. This relates to our duty to the government regarding taxes.
5. Reward the laborer. This is about the government's duty to the people.

  —*The Spiritual Laws of Life*, p. 13
  See also,
  —*The Secret of Love*, Mahanta Transcripts, Book 14, pp. 138–45

How is divine love expressed through each of these laws?

Five Passions of the Mind

1. Lust—Kama

Self-indulgence, one of the five passions of the mind, which is the principle of sickness and evil in the Kali Yuga; lust, or the degradation of sex; abnormal desire which includes drugs, alcoholic drinks, tobacco, or foods eaten only for taste. The antidote is one of the five virtues, discrimination.

Curbing any self-indulgence can help you with all forms of indulgence. Find out how that works.

2. Anger—Krodha

Tantrums, fury, mental carcinoma, slander, evil gossip, backbiting, profanity, faultfinding, jealousy, malice, impatience, resentment, mockery, destructive criticism, and ill will. The antidote is one of the five virtues, forgiveness and tolerance.

Create a spiritual technique to refrain from responding in anger. Use it in at least one instance today.

(Continued)

3. Greed—Lobha

   Miserliness, lying, hypocrisy, perjury, misrepresentation, robbery, bribery, and trickery of all sorts. The antidote is one of the five virtues, contentment.

   ———

   What is true spiritual contentment?

4. Vanity—Ahankara

   The abnormal exaggeration of the faculty of interest in self or the faculty of mind which gives the power of awareness of Soul; also self-righteousness; destroys all sense of humor; bigotry, self-assertion, obtrusive show of wealth or power, bossiness, scolding, faultfinding, liking publicity, making a show of religion, and being noisy about giving to charity; the opposite of humility, one of the five virtues, which is the antidote.

   ———

   Why can self-righteousness be so subtle? Grow alert to the signs.

(Continued)

5. Attachment—Moha

The state of being connected by ties of affection, attraction, etc., particularly to the karmic conditions of life that hold one in the physical universes; includes ideas, dreams, consciousness of the lower self which creates attachment to the physical realm, desires, and connections with family and possessions. The antidote is detachment, one of the five virtues.

Look for a new way to solve a stubborn problem.

—Adapted from *A Cosmic Sea of Words:
The ECKANKAR Lexicon*

Five Virtues

Practicing the five virtues of ECK—discrimination, tolerance and forgiveness, contentment, detachment, and humility—is a way to develop the spiritual intelligence of Soul. These virtues protect you from the snares of maya or illusion.

—*Spiritual Exercises for the Shariyat*, Book One, p. 37

1. Discrimination—Viveka

The ability to make right judgments; the recognition that there is no good nor evil, no beauty nor ugliness, no sin, and that these are concepts of the mind, the dual forces in the matter worlds; to distinguish between those actions which contribute to spiritual growth and those which are a waste of time. The remedy for self-indulgence, kama.

What could you add to or drop from your life to give yourself a spiritual boost?

2. Forgiveness and Tolerance—Kshama

Opposite of and the remedy for krodha, anger.

(Continued)

Is there anything in your life overdue for forgiveness? Try any act of charity toward another to build your momentum.

3. Contentment—Santosha

Peace and contentment; shanti, the peace of self which comes when one is rid of desire; a step on the path to the Far Country; the opposite of and remedy for lobha, or greed.

To take this step, let go of one unneeded desire, and replace it with peaceful acceptance.

4. Humility—Dinta

Opposite of vanity, ahankara, and the remedy for it; being humble, not proud or haughty.

Try practicing silence as a form of humility when an occasion arises.

5. Detachment—Vairag

Giving up strong affection for the environment and possessions, but not ceasing to identify with them; becoming independent of them; mentally free from love of the world and all worldly desires. The opposite of and remedy for moha, or attachment.

(Continued)

How do you balance detachment with responsibility?

—Adapted from *A Cosmic Sea of Words:
The ECKANKAR Lexicon*

ୢ

Five Keys to ECK Mastership

1. Give thanks for every gift, however small.

2. Be the best you can.

3. Do the best you can.

4. Love the gift of life.

5. Know that ECK is love.

—*Your Road Map to the ECK Teachings:
ECKANKAR Study Guide*, Vol. 2, p. 84

Try learning these by heart. Each key unlocks a greatness within you.

ୢ

Seven Margs

Paths to God

1. The Arahata Marg, the teaching order
2. The Bhakti Marg, the loving service order
3. The ECK Marg, secret path of the holy Sound Current
4. The Giani Marg, study at the Golden Wisdom Temples
5. The Karma Marg, similar to the Bhakti Marg, but of a more personal path of service to God
6. The Prapatti Marg, way of liberation via the Master
7. The Vahana Marg, the order of missionaries

In looking at these seven margs, it's quickly apparent how they blend into one another. There is a full harmony between them. Like waves in the ocean.

—Adapted from *Handbook for ECK Leaders*, pp. 162–63

Picture yourself in an ocean where each of these

(Continued)

waves of service and unfoldment wash over you, one at a time.

What is your next step?

☙

The Council of the Nine

The Council of the Nine are the ECK Masters responsible for the distribution of the ECK message in the lower worlds.

If spreading the teachings of ECK is your goal, then put attention upon these timeless ones during contemplation. Lay whatever problem you have on the line, and invite their help. Ask them to accompany you to work or ECK meetings.

Remember, no ECK Master will interfere with your plans unless given an express invitation. So you have to approach them during contemplation to request help formulating plans. Then be aware of them throughout your day.

This team of nine is unbeatable. Like the Sacketts of Louis L'Amour westerns, the brotherhood of ECK Adepts come from all spiritual regions to give help in the work of the Sugmad.

—*Ask the Master,* Book 1, pp. 191–92

How will you prepare yourself to work with the Council of the Nine?

Twelve-Year Cycles of the Master's Spiritual Mission

Era of Stabilization (1981–93)

In the first cycle, the ECK movement—and all the people in it—needed to learn what was right behavior and what was not. There is a responsibility to living here. . . .

Lessons learned in the first cycle included many topics. Among them: a code of ethical behavior, a better understanding of karma as a nonretributive part of spiritual law, divine love as the most powerful force in creation, and others.

—*Wisdom of the Heart*, Book 2, pp. 109–10

Is there something in your life that could benefit from stabilization? Contemplating on one of the topics given above may bring results.

(Continued)

Age of the ECK Missionary (1993–2005)

The lessons of the second cycle will become more evident—namely, how to bridge the gap between the ECK teachings and the spiritual needs of the people in today's society.

—*Wisdom of the Heart*, Book 2, p. 110

How do you bridge this gap for others?

A Time for Reaching Out (2005–17)

The creative spirit in ECK chelas will awaken to many so-far-undreamed-of ways to reach people ready for the wonderful teachings of ECK (the Holy Spirit).

—*The Mystic World*, December 2005, p. 6

It will include the aim of finding seekers, but now we will also look more into how to be of service where there are pressing spiritual needs.

—*RESA Star*, March 2006, p. 5

The Mahanta will show you new ways to awaken your creative spirit and reach a seeking Soul with divine love.

(Continued)

First of the Golden Years (2017–29)

We continue our search for Souls weary of illusions and help them return to God. Will you support this mission? If so, then rededicate your heart and hands to the Spirit Divine.

—*The Mystic World*, March 2018, p. 3

Watch for how life responds to your rededication. It surely will.

Second of the Golden Years (2029–41)

Third of the Golden Years (2041–53)

Fourth of the Golden Years (2053–65)

Fifth of the Golden Years (2065–77)

Sixth of the Golden Years (2077–89)

Seventh of the Golden Years (2089–2101)

Eighth of the Golden Years (2101–13)

Ninth of the Golden Years (2113–25)

Tenth of the Golden Years (2125–37)

Eleventh of the Golden Years (2137–49)

Twelfth of the Golden Years (2149–61)

The Spiritual Years of ECK

The year of ECK which begins on October 22 at midnight in the Valley of Tirmer.

—*A Cosmic Sea of Words: The ECKANKAR Lexicon*, p. 62

The Year of Light and Sound

The first year of the Spiritual Years of ECK. The Light and Sound, taken together, are the Voice of God, the Holy Spirit. They form a cosmic wave that goes out from the heart of God to the ends of creation. The Mahanta, the Living ECK Master's job is to help Soul learn to catch that wave which then flows home to God.

Picture yourself carried on a divine wave heading to the heart of God. You may hear any number of sounds, see any manner of Light.

(Continued)

A Year of Spiritual Healing

The second of the Spiritual Years of ECK. After spending many lifetimes in search of truth, the individual is often a bruised and battered wreck. So even after having bathed in the Light and Sound of God, Soul needs time to heal. So it is necessary to set aside a time of healing every twelve years for the individual to gather strength for the next leg of the spiritual journey.

What in your life helps you gather strength? Contemplation? Giving service? Patience? Find your answer, and give it some loving attention when times are hard.

The Year of the Shariyat

The third of the Spiritual Years of ECK. The Shariyat-Ki-Sugmad is the body of spiritual writings that form the ECK holy scriptures. These scriptures cut through the illusions of temporal power and lead Soul to wisdom, spiritual power, and freedom.

You can start a notebook or use a blank page at the end of the **Shariyat** *to create a personal index of favorite passages.*

(Continued)

Year of the ECK Missionary

The fourth of the Spiritual Years of ECK. Each Soul has a mission, a purpose. During this annual cycle, one tries to learn, then align, this personal mission with that of God's divine plan for each Soul's return home to God. Soul is here to learn divine love. Along the way, Soul learns that Its personal mission also means helping others find their way to it.

How do you see your day aligned with your personal mission?

A Year of HU

The fifth of the Spiritual Years of ECK. HU is the most ancient name for God, not God Itself. HU, the first impulse from the Ocean of Love and Mercy, is the original of all motion, force, light, sound, or vibration. Singing *HU* opens one to help from the Holy Spirit.

Make HU the first impulse of your day, your thoughts, your words and actions.

(Continued)

The Year of Giving

The sixth of the Spiritual Years of ECK. The entire reason for Soul's journey is to learn the spiritual need for giving. A life of meaning is a life of giving. God's love freely comes to all of us, so we must learn both to accept that love and then to pass it on to others.

Create time in your day for a special act of giving when the Inner Master shows you the need.

A Year of Blessing

The seventh of the Spiritual Years of ECK. A time to count your blessings. Bless each moment, each thought, each word, and each deed. Let only the pure love of God flow from you and into your own universe.

Your heart may soften and glow warm with love as you begin to count your blessings. Another blessing.

(Continued)

The Year of Thanksgiving

The eighth of the Spiritual Years of ECK. This year has much in common with A Year of Blessing, which precedes it. We must be willing to let our joy of life show in a spirit of celebration. Enjoy the company of your loved ones at special celebrations of your own choosing throughout the year. Give thanks for the gift of life.

Sharing your joy for life is a blessing to others.

A Year of Creativity

The ninth of the Spiritual Years of ECK. God's special gift to the higher forms of spiritual evolution is the gift of creativity. It is a reflection of Soul's highest nature.

How will you use this gift today? Solving a problem? Repairing a relationship? Preparing a meal?

(Continued)

Year of the ECK Teacher

The tenth of the Spiritual Years of ECK. This year is opposite on the wheel to its counterpart, Year of the ECK Missionary. First, the missionary finds the Souls that are ready for the return home to God. Later, the ECK teacher, the Arahata, as an aide to the Mahanta, the Living ECK Master, leads a class of people who desire the knowledge of truth found in the ECK teachings. This is a key year.

What can others learn about ECK through your example? Through how you deal with change or conflict?

The Year of Graceful Living

The eleventh of the Spiritual Years of ECK. As Souls unfold, their way of interacting with others becomes more graceful. There is an honest attempt to see the Mahanta in every Soul, because then a graceful life is found to be the natural life. Grace is a balm that makes things run better.

What does being graceful mean to you?

(Continued)

A Year of Consecration

The twelfth of the Spiritual Years of ECK. A time to dedicate oneself anew to *being* a Co-worker with God. A chance to tie up loose spiritual ends of the last cycle and prepare for the new one next year.

In whatever way is right for you, rededicate yourself to your journey to the heart of God.

—Adapted from *A Cosmic Sea of Words: The ECKANKAR Lexicon*

The Creation of Life

He must think of ECK as life. It is that essence, that fluid, or Holy Spirit which flows out of God to be used as the creative force for the feeding and maintenance of all things in every universe of the Sugmad, whether it be a piece of mineral, a particle of soil, an animal, or a man.

All the same, It is the basic reality, the chain of invisible atoms that man breathes for survival in the flesh, that he uses to create thought, that is the basic but necessary element by which life is created and maintained. It cannot be anything else but this, and when It is viewed from the eyes of Soul, or what is often called the esoteric viewpoint or the viewpoint of the Atma Sarup, It appears to be simply a great, radiant sheet of blazing light, too great for the human sight, stretching from infinity to infinity, without a beginning, without an ending. It sometimes appears like a great, calm, brooding sea, reflecting a thousand times the light of a brilliant sun. This is the consciousness of the Mahanta, the Living ECK Master.

—*The Shariyat-Ki-Sugmad*, Books One & Two, pp. 384–85

(Continued)

Draw your next breath with wonder and gratitude for God's love for you.

∽

Liberation of HU

Rebazar Tarzs once said, "Let your faith, your inner trust and confidence stream forth; remove your inner obstacles and open yourself to truth." It is this kind of faith, or inner awareness and open-mindedness, which finds its spontaneous expression, its liberation from an overwhelming psychic pressure, in the sacred sound of the HU. In this mantric sound all the positive and forward-pressing forces of the human, which are trying to blow up its limitations and burst the fetters of ignorance, are united and concentrated on the ECK, like an arrow point.

—*The Shariyat-Ki-Sugmad*, Books One & Two, p. 333

When you encounter obstacles, pressure, limitation, or ignorance, remember to chant HU *with confidence and an open mind.*

∽

Goodness like Water

The highest goodness in man, like water, is characterized by humility. A good man or a good king is self-effacing, like the ECK. Consequently, his object is peace; and the picture of peace consists of families secure on their land and the people thoughtful, kind, and sincere.

All must be able to control their animal nature enough to be pure in heart, never distracted from the way of ECK. Each person must be capable of personal discipline that will enable him to love unselfishly, wield virtue, and, at last, understand all, while denying himself. He must put life into others without trying to own them. He must never depend upon anyone. He can be the king, but never the tyrant. This is what the ECK requires of all people.

—*The Shariyat-Ki-Sugmad,*
Books One & Two, p. 415

Consider what it means to "put life into others."
This is something between you and the Inner Master.

The Master's Gift

Complete surrender means that out of perfect confidence and a great love, the chela will gladly follow where the Living ECK Master leads him. By giving himself up to the Living ECK Master, in this sense, the chela gains everything, which ends in perfect liberty in the spiritual worlds. Yaubl Sacabi stated, "Give the ECK Master all that you have, and he will give you all he possesses!"

—*The Shariyat-Ki-Sugmad*,
Books One & Two, p. 131

Today there will be at least one perfectly clear choice you can make to follow the Mahanta gladly.

Every Moment

At the heart of the ECK life lies the conviction that the ECK is the way as well as the goal. Therefore, whether the way is long or short, and whatever blind corners it has, every moment is as important as the goal. It is only because to live as the Mahanta that to die is to gain.

In practical terms this means that every moment is known to be of infinite value, not because of what precedes or follows it, but because it is the moment of communication with God, in which eternity is a present reality as one holds and possesses the whole fullness of life in one moment, here and now, the past, present, and future.

—*The Shariyat-Ki-Sugmad*,
Books One & Two, p. 363

This very moment is as important as your goal of God-Realization. Take this to heart.

Lai Tsi's Prayer

Show me Thy ways, O Sugmad;

Teach me Thy path.

Lead me in Thy truth, and teach me;

On Thee do I wait all day.

Remember, O Beloved, Thy guiding light

And Thy loving care.

For it has been ever Thy will,

To lead the least of Thy servants to Thee!

—*The Shariyat-Ki-Sugmad*,
Books One & Two, pp. 404–5

Learn this by heart so it will be at the ready anytime there is a need for guidance, comfort, upliftment.

৯

Marks of the ECK Leader

The ECK leader is an agent for the ECK.

He shows the world the unmatched power of the spiritual exercises to lift the human consciousness. Light and Sound, the twin aspects of God, are the only door to freedom.

He walks the most direct path to God and presents the ECK teachings simply, without criticizing another's beliefs. Strongly anchored upon the ECK Life Stream, he keeps the ECK programs from drifting into curious debates on psychic phenomena. He teaches only the laws of truth and Spirit.

The leader in ECK treats everyone with respect and dignity, for each person is a particle of God. Regard for Soul's sanctity allows him to let others be themselves.

In conversation with an inquirer, the ECK leader listens with care, puts himself into the other person's place and, without probing, opens the discussion to spiritual things that play upon the mind.

Curiosity about a searcher's opinion gives him the compassion to understand Soul's contest to break free

(Continued)

from the downward pull of base materialism. Humble service to the SUGMAD, in love, bears its own reward.

The ECK leader knows the purpose of his being is service, not self-glorification.

Sensitive to the feelings of others, he greets visitors to the ECK Center and public events in a warm and cordial manner.

Respecting the seeker's privacy, he offers to tell him about the ECK programs in the community.

These are a few of the marks of an ECK leader.

—Adapted from *The Mystic World*,
Summer, 1984

The way you live your daily life can teach others the laws of truth and Spirit. Be a light unto the world.

৯

ECK *Parables*
Essential Stories to Live By

The Scratched Diamond

This is "The Scratched Diamond" from *The Hungry Clothes and Other Jewish Folktales* retold by Peninnah Schram. Here it's being retold by me.

A student was walking along with his master one day. This master was known for always answering questions with a parable. His student said, "Rabbi, I have so many imperfections. What can I do? How can I work with them so that I can be a better person?" The Rabbi said, "Listen, and I'll tell you a story.

"There was once a king, and he had a beautiful diamond without a flaw—not a single flaw anywhere. You could turn it in the light, and it just sparkled. The facets all sparkled in an expected way, and when dignitaries came over, the king would show them his priceless diamond. He was so proud of it. Dignitaries would say, 'We're going to have to see His Majesty's diamond again.' 'That's OK, just make believe you enjoy it.'

"They would go in and say, 'Oh, wow! Yep, sure is good. As pretty as can be. Just the same as last time.'

(Continued)

"But one day the king looked at it, and he noticed there was a scratch on it. Maybe he had been tossing it around with his other jewels, and he shouldn't have done that. Anyway, it had a flaw now. But he had an ace up his sleeve.

"He called in the best diamond cutters in the kingdom. And he said, 'All right, you guys. You're the best there is. What can you do to restore this diamond?'

"Then one by one they took it, looked at it, and said, 'Your Majesty, there isn't a blessed thing we can do to restore this diamond to its original condition.'

"But standing by, looking on, was a young diamond cutter. He just finished his apprenticeship with the best diamond cutter in the kingdom, and he asked the king, 'May I look at that?' The king said, 'Sure. Why not?' The young man looked at it. He studied it very carefully, and he said, 'If you will allow me to take it with me and to work uninterrupted, never asking for updates or anything, I'm going to try to make it a thing of worth and value.'

"Well, what's a king to do? He had a lot of other jewelry. This diamond was worth as much as all the rest of his jewelry. When you've got a lot, you don't care a lot. Unless you don't have a lot anymore, like

(Continued)

it's all gone all of a sudden. But he wasn't faced with that kind of problem.

"So this young craftsman went to work on it with all his love, because he loved his craft. Because it takes a great deal of skill and dexterity and vision. You've got to have vision to create something unusual and something from nothing.

"When he brought the diamond back to the king, the king looked at it, and he was amazed. He was delighted. And he said, 'You did this to it?' And what did he do to it?

"Well, when the young man had looked at the diamond, he saw the scratch as the stem of a rose. Very carefully he etched roots onto the stem, and then leaves onto the stem, and then a flower onto the stem. From the scratch he had created a thing of beauty and value. In fact, it was more beautiful and more valuable to the king now than it had ever been."

When the Rabbi finished his story, he looked at his student and said, "We all have our faults and failings. But, like the diamond with its scratch, it's up to us to transform them into things of beauty and value."

—*The Master's Talks in The Year of Light and Sound—2013–14*, pp. 27–29

ஒ

"Turn the Carpet" or "The Two Weavers"

This was written by Hannah More.

As at their work two Weavers sat,
Beguiling time with friendly chat;
They touched upon the price of meat,
So high, a Weaver scarce could eat.

What with my brats and sickly wife,
Quoth Dick, I'm almost tired of life;
So hard my work, so poor my fare,
`Tis more than mortal man can bear.

How glorious is the rich man's state!
His house so fine! His wealth so great
Heaven is unjust you must agree,
Why all to him, why none to me?

In spite of what the Scripture teaches,
In spite of all the Parson preaches,
This world (indeed I've thought so long)
Is ruled, methinks, extremely wrong.

Wheree'er I look, howe'er I range,
`Tis all confused, and hard, and strange;
The good are troubled and oppressed,
And all the wicked are the blessed.

(Continued)

*O*ur ignorance is the cause, said John,
Why thus we blame our Maker's laws;
Parts of his ways alone we know,
`Tis all that man can see below.

*S*ee'st thou that Carpet, not half done,
Which thou, dear Dick, hast well begun?
Behold the wild confusion there,
So rude the mass it makes one stare!

A stranger, ignorant of the trade,
Would say, no meaning's there conveyed;
For where's the middle, where's the border
Thy Carpet now is all disorder.

*Q*uoth Dick, my work is yet in bits,
But still in every part it fits;
Besides, you reason like a lout,
Why, man, that *Carpet's inside out*.

*S*ays John, thou say'st the thing I mean,
and now I hope to cure thy spleen;
This world, which clouds thy soul with doubt,
Is but a Carpet inside out.

*A*nd when we view these shreds and ends,
We know not what the whole intends;
So when on earth things seem but odd,
They're working still some scheme of God.

(Continued)

No plan, no pattern can we trace,
All wants proportion, truth, and grace;
The motley mixture we deride,
Nor see the beauteous upper side.

But when we reach that world of light,
And view these works of God aright;
Then shall we see the whole design,
And own the workman is divine.

What now seem random strokes, will there
All order and design appear;
Then shall we praise what here we spurned,
For then the *Carpet shall be turned*.

Thou'st right, quoth Dick, no more I'll grumble,
That this sad world's so strange a jumble;
My impious doubts are put to flight,
For my own Carpet sets me right.

* * *

When we see the shreds and ends of our own lives, turn the carpet. Look on the other side. See what's there. See the beauty that speaks to the handiwork of the creator.

—*The Master's Talks in The Year of Light and Sound—2013–14*, pp. 24–26, 29

The Zen Master

There was a Zen master. He had a small band of followers who looked to him for guidance. One of them had a small son. This son wanted a horse very badly. So, after some time, the parents were able to get the money together, and they got him a horse.

His friends said, "That's good!" But the Zen master said, "We'll see."

Some years later, when he was fifteen years old, the young man was riding his horse. As he was riding, he fell off and broke his leg. It mended poorly so that he always walked with a limp.

His friends said, "That's bad." The Zen master said, "We'll see."

Then war broke out. Anybody who was eligible to be drafted was drafted. Young men from the neighborhood all had to go, except for this young man who had injured himself during the fall from his horse.

(Continued)

So when the neighbors and friends heard that the young man was exempt because of his leg, they said, "That's wonderful!" The Zen master said, "We'll see."

—The Master's Talks in A Year of Blessing—2007–8, pp. 9–10

℘

The Master Brush Cleaner

There was once a painter whose art was renowned for its great beauty. People would cry, being so moved by the exquisite relationship between the paint, the canvas, and the subject matter. Color, texture, light, and perspective created a unique harmonic beauty like a great piece of music or a majestic voice.

His paintings had such power!

All this was due to the fact that he was a master brush cleaner. The deep love, joy, and care he put into tending his brushes manifested in his art. The love became these beautiful paintings. People would come to study with him, in hopes of discovering his painting technique. They saw he spent a lot of time cleaning and caring for his brushes, and many—most—thought that was just his eccentric, tiresome routine.

Oiling the brush handles, conditioning the bristles.

Some thought it his superstition; others, that he was somewhat mad. Yet occasionally, students searching

(Continued)

out his secrets would imitate his brush-cleaning process, but they did not love their brushes. When someone would ask why he spent (wasted) so much time cleaning his brushes, he would just smile and shrug.

Students would endlessly watch him paint but would barely notice the brushes luxuriating in the pots of color, dancing with the chance to come alive with their highest potential in the hands of one who loved them.

The canvas begged for his strokes.

Incredibly rare that a student would catch the secret that it was in the care of the brushes. But when that student came, it brought the painter a transcendent joy. The student had caught the secret that the brushes were not magical. The painter was not magical. But the love was. It was not the technique. It was in the investment in the Source.

The painter did not care whether the people loved the paintings. He only cared that they brought him students. And maybe one of them would come to know and embody this secret of love himself. The student would then have the secret of life!

This is a classic story.

—*The Wisdom Notes*, June 2016

"One Does What One Can"

A horseman was riding along a road, and far up ahead he sees something lying right smack in the middle of the road. So he goes up there, and he sees it's a little sparrow, lying on its back. He says, "Are you hurt?" The little sparrow says, "No."

The rider asks, "Well then, what are you lying on your back like that for?" The little bird says, "Well, I heard the sky is going to fall today." The horseman laughs and says, "Well, that's foolish. You think you could hold up the whole sky with your spindly little legs?"

The little bird says, "One does what one can."

—*The Master's Talks in A Year of Spiritual Healing*—2014–15, pp. 2–3

The Jade Master

"The Jade Master" is a story in a book by Ed Seykota called *The Trader's Window*. It's about a young man who didn't know what to do with his life.

He had heard about a man known as the jade master who lived about five miles away. One day the young man said to himself, *Even though it's winter, I'm going to visit the jade master and learn all about jade.*

So he walks five miles through the snow and bitter cold. Finally he comes to the jade master's house and knocks on the door. An old man with a broom in his hand opens it. "Yes? What can I do for you?"

The young man says, "I've come to learn about jade. Would you take me as your student?"

"Sure," the old man says. "Come on in."

Inside the house the jade master makes the young man a cup of green tea, then presses a green stone

(Continued)

into his hand. "Hold that while we talk," he says. And as they sip their tea on this cold winter day, the old man begins telling a story about a green tree frog.

The young man becomes very impatient. He doesn't want to hear about tree frogs. "Excuse me," he says, "I came here to learn about jade."

"Oh, excuse me," the old man said. "Why don't you come back next week?"

Puzzled, the young man heads for home. The following week he trudges all the way back through five miles of cold snow. The old man opens the door and lets him in. He makes the hot tea, presses this green stone into the student's hand, and again begins to talk about a green tree frog.

This time the young man is able to listen a little bit longer. Finally he says, "Excuse me, but I came here to learn about jade." He thinks the old man is going senile on him.

"Oh, excuse me," the jade master says. "Maybe you'd better just go home now and come back next week."

This went on all winter long, and each time the young man returned, he would interrupt the jade master less and less. In the meantime, he learned a

(Continued)

few things. He now knew how to make green tea and how to sweep the kitchen floor with the broom. As he and the old man became friends, he began to make himself useful and help with the things that needed to be done.

As always, the old man would sit down and start talking about the green tree frog. The young man just listened now, never interrupting until the old man got tired. Then he would trudge home through five miles of snow and come back the following week.

One day he arrived for his weekly visit. It was spring now, much easier to make the five-mile walk. The jade master opened the door and told him to come in. As the student sat down, the old man pressed the green stone into his hand and gave him a cup of green tea. Again he began to tell the story of the green tree frog.

"Wait a minute," the young man said. "This isn't jade." Suddenly he knew that the green stone in his hand wasn't jade.

Maybe I shouldn't explain it. Maybe I shouldn't say that the green stone is truth. Maybe the stories I tell you have no more to do with anything than the old man's story about the green tree frog. Yet what is

(Continued)

it that I put in your hand? The Spiritual Exercises of ECK, the word *HU*.

What you need to realize is that HU is a priceless gem, the most beautiful of prayers, a love song to God.

And how do you do it?

You just sing *HU* every day. Just as the jade master pressed this green stone into the young man's hand, the Mahanta, the Inner Master, presses the spiritual exercise with the word *HU* to your heart every day. But you have to take it to heart, and then go about your business.

Go about your daily life. Drink the green tea, listen to people tell their stories about the green tree frog. And wherever you are, do the things that are necessary: bring in the wood, bring home the groceries, sweep the floor.

Do these things, and someday you will find that you have the secret of truth in your hand, but better: you will have the secret of truth in your heart.

—Adapted from *How the Inner Master Works*, Mahanta Transcripts, Book 12, pp. 106–9

The God Seeker

This is an insight into the masses of people who are really looking for nothing higher than the Cosmic Consciousness—and the few truly seeking God.

The Cosmic Consciousness seekers sit in a huge audience watching actors on stage direct their spiritual searching for them. Reading wise words on printed paper, the actors are wrapped up only in matters that titillate the mind with beauty and other wonders.

The God Seeker is not part of that huge crowd. He does not sit respectfully in a well-mannered and sophisticated theater audience, but crawls through the dust of life on his belly, like a swimmer in the ocean.

(Continued)

The man intent on God Consciousness is humble, and those in the audience eye him as a simpleton. But he crawls in a straight line toward his goal, skirting the platform being paced by actors with clever words. He strikes out instead toward a region beyond, an area not considered worthwhile to the average seeker.

And the Unchangeable Law of God, of the Sugmad, has him in Its relentless grip.

—*The Mystic World*, June 2015, p. 2

About the Author

Author Harold Klemp is known as a pioneer of today's focus on "everyday spirituality." He was raised on a Wisconsin farm and attended divinity school. He also served in the US Air Force.

In 1981, after lifetimes of training, he became the spiritual leader of Eckankar, the Path of Spiritual Freedom. His full title is Sri Harold Klemp, the Mahanta, the Living ECK Master. His mission is to help people find their way back to God in this life.

Each year, Harold Klemp speaks to thousands of seekers at Eckankar seminars. Author of more than one hundred books, he continues to write, including many articles and spiritual-study discourses. His inspiring and practical approach to spirituality helps many thousands of people worldwide find greater freedom, wisdom, and love in their lives.

Advanced Spiritual Living

Go higher, further, deeper with your spiritual exploration!

ECK membership brings many unique benefits and a focus on the ECK discourses. These are dynamic spiritual courses you study at home, one per month.

The first year of study brings *The Easy Way Discourses* by Harold Klemp, with uplifting spiritual exercises, audio excerpts from his seminar talks, and activities to personalize your spiritual journey. Classes are available in many areas.

Each year you choose to continue with ECK membership can bring new levels of divine freedom, inner strength to meet the challenges of life, and direct experience with the love and power of God.

Here's a sampling of titles from *The Easy Way Discourses:*

- In Soul You Are Free
- Reincarnation—Why You Came to Earth Again
- The Master Principle
- The God Worlds—Where No One Has Gone Before?

How to Get Started

For free books and more information about Eckankar:

- Visit www.Eckankar.org;
- Call 1-800-LOVE GOD (1-800-568-3463) (USA and Canada only); or
- Write to: ECKANKAR, Dept. BK 132, PO Box 2000, Chanhassen, MN 55317-2000 USA.

To order Eckankar books online, you can visit www.ECKBooks.org.

To receive your advanced spiritual-study discourses, along with other annual membership benefits, go to www.Eckankar.org (click on "Membership" then "Online Membership Application"). You can also call Eckankar at (952) 380-2222 to apply. Or write to the address above, Att: Membership.

For Further Reading and Study

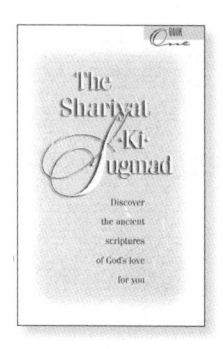

The Shariyat-Ki-Sugmad, Books One and Two

The "Way of the Eternal." These writings are the scriptures of ECKANKAR. They speak to you directly and come alive in your heart.

A Cosmic Sea of Words: The ECKANKAR Lexicon

The ultimate companion book for all Eckankar literature. An easy-to-use guide to over 1,900 key spiritual terms and concepts for today's reader.

The Mahanta Transcripts Series
Harold Klemp

The Mahanta Transcripts, books 1–17, are from Harold Klemp's talks at Eckankar seminars. He has taught thousands how to have a natural, direct relationship with the Holy Spirit. The stories and wonderful insights contained in these talks will lead you to deeper spiritual understanding.

Book 17

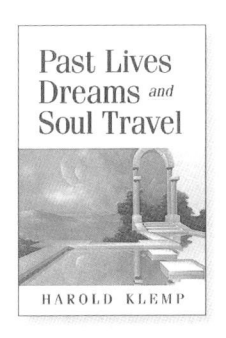

Past Lives, Dreams, and Soul Travel
Harold Klemp

These stories and exercises help you find your true purpose, discover greater love than you've ever known, and learn that spiritual freedom is within reach.

The Spiritual Exercises of ECK
Harold Klemp

This book is a staircase with 131 steps leading to the doorway to spiritual freedom, self-mastery, wisdom, and love. A comprehensive volume of spiritual exercises for every need.

Autobiography of a Modern Prophet
Harold Klemp

This riveting story of Harold Klemp's climb up the Mountain of God will help you discover the keys to your own spiritual greatness.

Glossary

Words set in SMALL CAPS are defined elsewhere in this glossary.

Blue Light How the MAHANTA often appears in the inner worlds to the chela or seeker.

ECK The Life Force, the Holy Spirit, or Audible Life Current which sustains all life.

Eckankar *EHK-ahn-kahr* The Path of Spiritual Freedom. Also known as the Ancient Science of SOUL TRAVEL. A truly spiritual way of life for the individual in modern times. The teachings provide a framework for anyone to explore their own spiritual experiences. Established by PAUL TWITCHELL, the modern-day founder, in 1965. The word means Co-worker with God.

ECK Masters Spiritual Masters who can assist and protect people in their spiritual studies and travels. The ECK Masters are from a long line of God-Realized SOULS who know the responsibility that goes with spiritual freedom.

God-Realization The state of God Consciousness. Complete and conscious awareness of God.

HU *HYOO* The most ancient, secret name for God. The singing of the word *HU* is considered a love song to God. It can be sung aloud or silently to oneself to align with God's love.

Kal Niranjan *KAL nee-RAHN-jahn* The Kal Niranjan is the negative manifestation of God through which the power flows to sustain the lower universes; personification of the negative.

Klemp, Harold The present MAHANTA, the LIVING ECK MASTER. SRI Harold Klemp became the Mahanta, the Living ECK Master in 1981. His spiritual name is WAH Z.

Living ECK Master The title of the spiritual leader of ECKANKAR. He leads SOUL back to God. He teaches in the physical world as the Outer Master, in the dream state as the Dream Master, and in the spiritual worlds as the Inner Master. SRI HAROLD KLEMP became the MAHANTA, the Living ECK Master in 1981.

Mahanta An expression of the Spirit of God that is always with you.

Sometimes seen as a BLUE LIGHT or Blue Star or in the form of the Mahanta, the LIVING ECK MASTER. The highest state of God Consciousness on earth, only embodied in the Living ECK Master. He is the Living Word.

planes Levels of existence, such as the Physical, Astral, Causal, Mental, Etheric, and SOUL Planes.

Rebazar Tarzs A Tibetan ECK MASTER known as the Torchbearer of ECKANKAR in the lower worlds.

Self-Realization SOUL recognition. The entering of Soul into the Soul PLANE and there beholding Itself as pure Spirit. A state of seeing, knowing, and being.

Shariyat-Ki-Sugmad The sacred scriptures of ECKANKAR. The scriptures are comprised of twelve volumes in the spiritual worlds. The first two were transcribed from the inner PLANES by PAUL TWITCHELL, modern-day founder of Eckankar.

Soul The True Self, an individual, eternal spark of God. The inner, most sacred part of each person. Soul can see, know, and perceive all things. It is the creative center of Its own world.

Soul Travel The expansion of consciousness. The ability of SOUL to transcend the physical body and travel into the spiritual worlds of God. Soul Travel is taught only by the LIVING ECK MASTER. It helps people unfold spiritually and can provide proof of the existence of God and life after death.

Sound and Light of ECK The Holy Spirit. The two aspects through which God appears in the lower worlds. People can experience them by looking and listening within themselves and through SOUL TRAVEL.

Spiritual Exercises of ECK Daily practices for direct, personal experiences with the Sound Current. Creative techniques using contemplation and the singing of sacred words to bring the higher awareness of SOUL into daily life.

Sri *SREE* A title of spiritual respect, similar to reverend or pastor, used for those who have attained the Kingdom of God. In ECKANKAR, it is reserved for the MAHANTA, the LIVING ECK MASTER.

Sugmad *SOOG-mahd* A sacred name for God. It is the source of all life, neither male nor female, the Ocean of Love and Mercy.

Twitchell, Paul   An American ECK MASTER who brought the modern teachings of ECKANKAR to the world through his writings and lectures. His spiritual name is Peddar Zaskq.

Wah Z   *WAH zee*   The spiritual name of SRI HAROLD KLEMP. It means the secret doctrine. It is his name in the spiritual worlds.

For more explanations of ECKANKAR terms, see *A Cosmic Sea of Words: The ECKANKAR Lexicon* by Harold Klemp.